Mr. Gilmore's Glasses

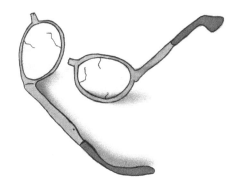

Based on a true story

To: Brady,
Life long blessings,
Heath Smith

Heath Smith

ISBN 978-1-64458-421-7 (paperback)
ISBN 978-1-64458-422-4 (digital)

Christian Faith Publishing, Inc.
832 Park Avenue
Meadville, PA 16335
www.christianfaithpublishing.com

Printed in the United States of America

To my dearest friends Debbie and Donna,
thank you for this story, your infectious smiles,
contagious laughs, and especially Friday nights for
which my life has truly been blessed as a result.

1

Debbie and Donna are sisters who live on a small farm with their momma and daddy and many cats. They love to play outside and often get into mischief.

One day they decided to go with their dad to visit Mr. Gilmore. He was a kind man, and the sisters loved to see his fascinating workshop. Mr. Gilmore's big blue work truck was parked under a shed outside.

"Let's go pretend to drive Mr. Gilmore's truck," said Debbie.

"Okay," Donna replied, "but I get to drive first."

They climbed up into the cab of the big truck. It was dusty and full of spider webs. While investigating inside, Debbie noticed a compartment. *I wonder what's in here?* Debbie thought. She opened the compartment, and there was a pair of glasses. They were an aged golden yellow and very scratched. She grabbed the glasses and tried them on.

"Look, Donna, I'm wearing Mr. Gilmore's glasses!"

"You look funny!" said Donna.

After wearing Mr. Gilmore's glasses for a while, Debbie reached to take them off. But when she did, they broke!

"Oooo! You broke Mr. Gilmore's glasses!" Donna said.

"I didn't mean to," replied Debbie.

"I'm telling Daddy as soon as he comes out here that you broke Mr. Gilmore's glasses."

"Oh, please don't!" Debbie pleaded.

"Fine," Donna answered. "But you have to do everything I say from now on, or I'll tell Daddy you broke Mr. Gilmore's glasses!"

Debbie replied reluctantly, "Okay."

A few days passed, and Donna was in her room bored stiff. She yelled to Debbie, "Come play Monopoly with me."

"I don't want to," Debbie yelled back.

"If you don't come play with me, I'll tell Daddy you broke Mr. Gilmore's glasses!"

Knowing she would get into trouble if Donna told, Debbie agreed to play Monopoly.

The following week, Donna wanted to go play in the creek that flowed behind the house.

"Let's go play in the creek, Debbie."

Debbie responded, "I'm tired, and the water is too cold! Can we go another day?"

"If you don't come play in the creek with me, I'll tell Daddy you broke Mr. Gilmore's glasses."

Debbie was very angry. "Fine!"

So they went to play and splash in the creek.

After a couple of weeks of Donna's saying she would tell on Debbie if she didn't do what she said, Debbie had had enough. One evening, while riding home in the car, Donna whispered to Debbie, "If you don't play dolls with me when we get home, I'll tell…"

"*YES*, I broke Mr. Gilmore's glasses!" Debbie shouted.

Donna was surprised that her sister had just told on herself.

Debbie cried, "I didn't mean to break them, Daddy. It was an accident!"

When they arrived to their house, their daddy called Mr. Gilmore to ask about the glasses. Debbie was frightened of what her daddy would say, but when he hung up the telephone, he reassured her, "It's all right. Mr. Gilmore said they were an old pair of glasses, that he was not using anymore.

But you should always remember that you are never supposed to touch anything that isn't yours without asking first."

"Okay, Daddy, I'm sorry,"
Debbie answered.

Later that evening, while lying in bed, Donna turned to Debbie, "I'm sorry for being so mean to you about breaking the glasses. I selfishly used your mistake to get what I wanted."

21

"It's okay," Debbie replied. "You're my sister, and I will always love you."

22

Debbie and Donna still quite often get into mischief, but whenever they visit Mr. Gilmore's and play in his big work truck, they are ever mindful of what they touch, especially if it's a pair of glasses.

About the Author

Heath Smith is a first-time author and illustrator. Having a true passion for children, it is without question that his first publication be a children's book. Heath quoted, "Every person on the planet was at one time a child. Every child has a story. In this particular case, it was two of my dearest friends whose recollection of a time in their childhood inspired this funny but very true story."

Outside of writing, Heath works as an interior and floral designer, creating unique spaces and one-of-a-kind arrangements. "I find that design, writing, and illustrating allows one to create environments that capture the attention of the beholder." *Mr. Gilmore's Glasses* is the first publication in a bright literary future for author Heath Smith.

CPSIA information can be obtained
at www.ICGtesting.com
Printed in the USA
BVHW021759230419
546307BV00001B/1/P